draw

This sketch pad belongs to

----

sky blue drawing pad for kids
walapie media | trendy wares misc.
copyright 2018

Get ready to

draw!

Use the drawing prompts on each page to help you draw

OR

Draw whatever you want!

TRY DRAWING A CIRCLE

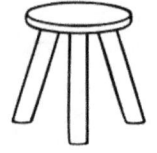
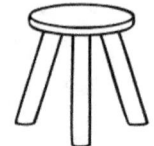
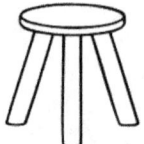
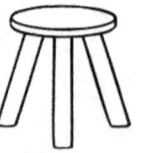

TRY DRAWING A CHAIR

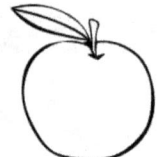

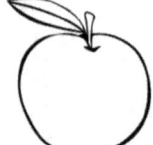
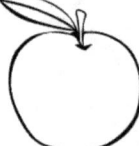

TRY DRAWING AN APPLE

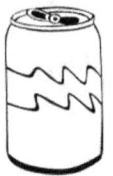
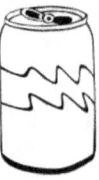
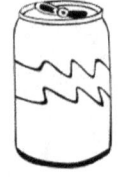
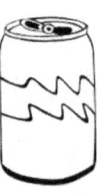

TRY DRAWING A SODA CAN

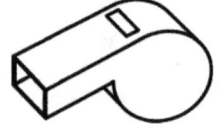
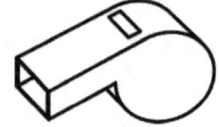
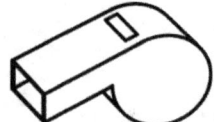
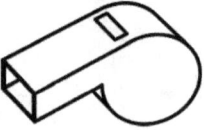

TRY DRAWING A WHISTLE

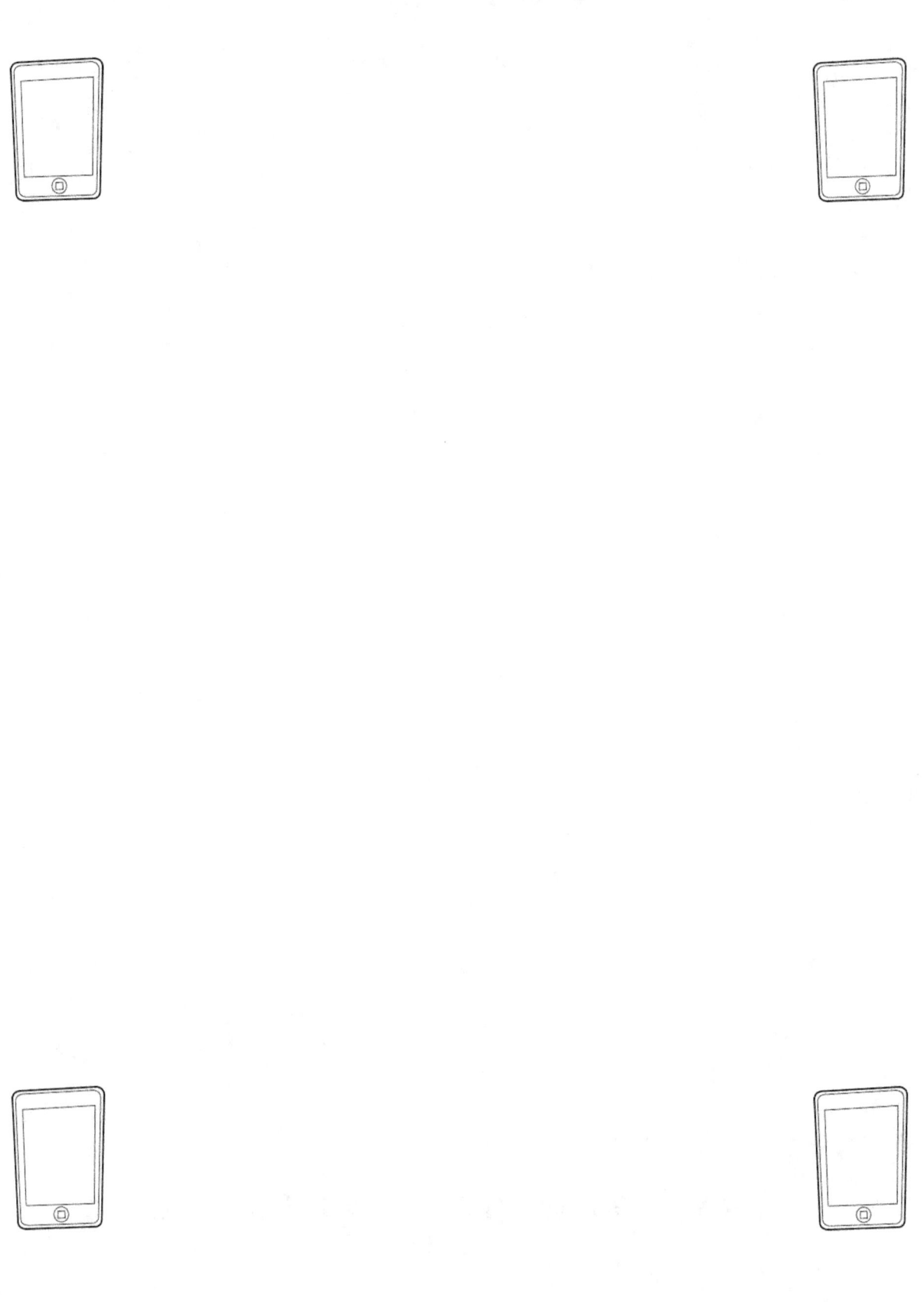

TRY DRAWING A CELL PHONE

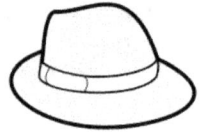
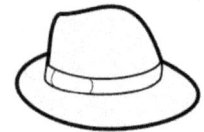
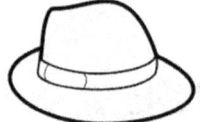
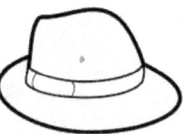

TRY DRAWING A HAT

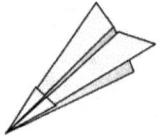
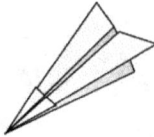
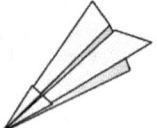
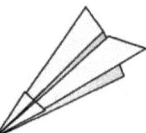

TRY DRAWING A PAPER AIRPLANE

TRY DRAWING A PENCIL

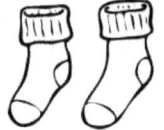
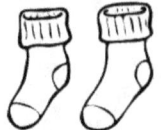
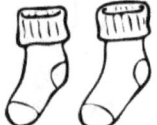
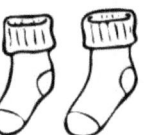

TRY DRAWING SOCKS

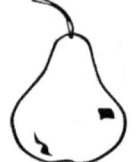
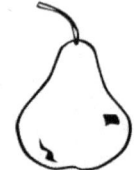
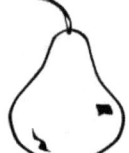
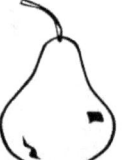

TRY DRAWING A PEAR

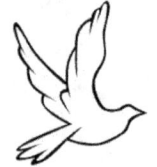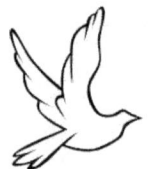

TRY DRAWING A DOVE

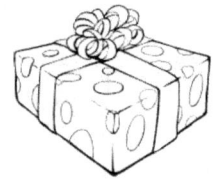
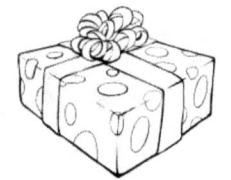
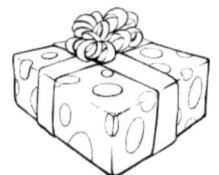
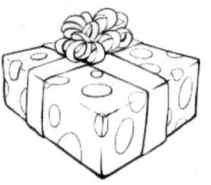

TRY DRAWING A PRESENT

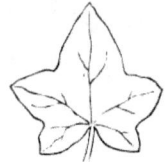
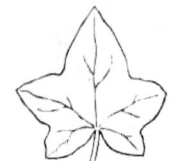
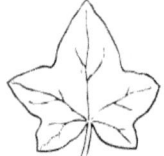
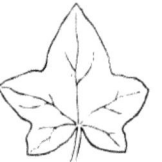

TRY DRAWING AN IVY LEAF

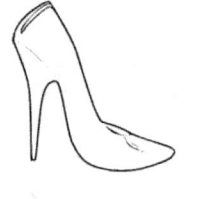
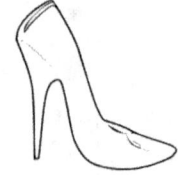
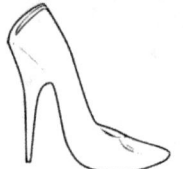
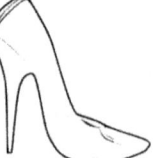

TRY DRAWING A HIGH HEEL

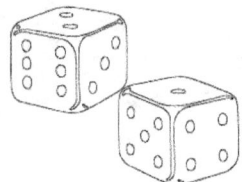

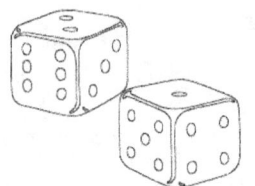

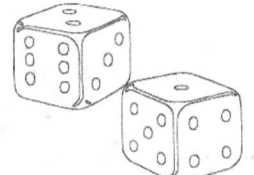

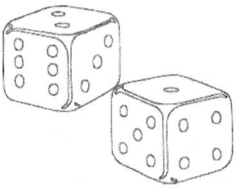

TRY DRAWING DICE

TRY DRAWING THE SUN

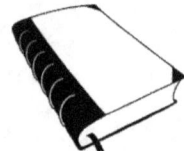
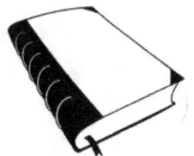
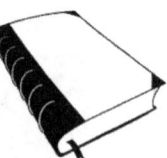

TRY DRAWING A CLOSED BOOK

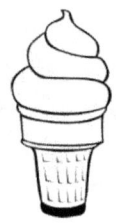
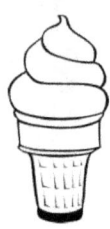
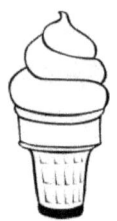
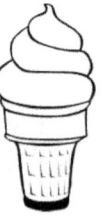

TRY DRAWING AN ICE CREAM CONE

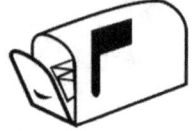
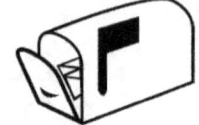
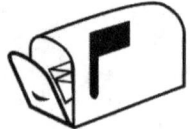
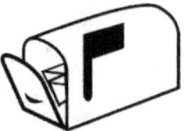

TRY DRAWING A MAILBOX

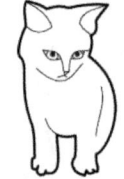
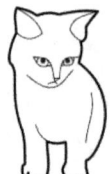
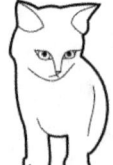
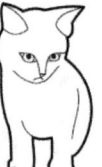

TRY DRAWING A CAT

TRY DRAWING A DRUM

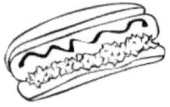
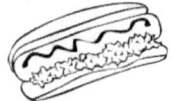
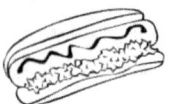
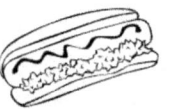

TRY DRAWING A HOT DOG

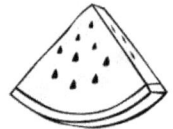
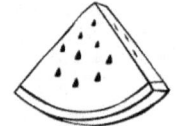
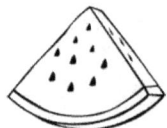
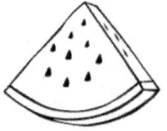

TRY DRAWING A WATERMELON

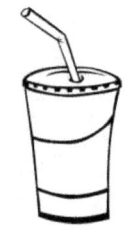
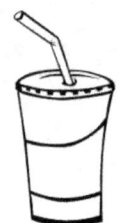
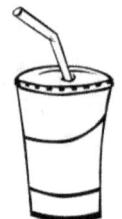
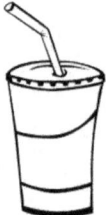

TRY DRAWING A CUP

TRY DRAWING A FLOWER

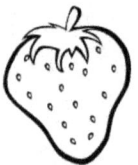

TRY DRAWING A STRAWBERRY

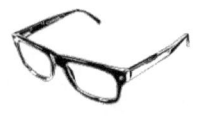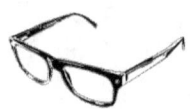

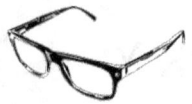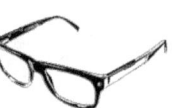

TRY DRAWING GLASSES

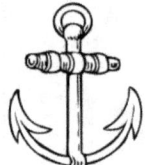
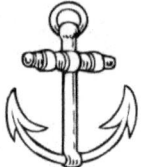
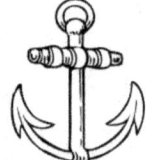
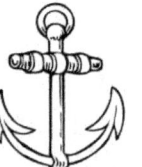

TRY DRAWING AN ANCHOR

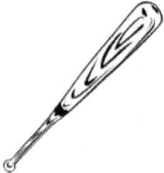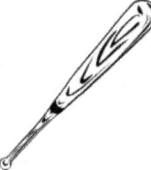

TRY DRAWING A BASEBALL BAT

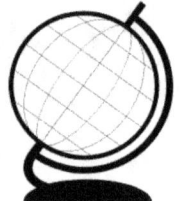
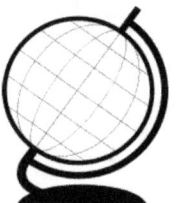
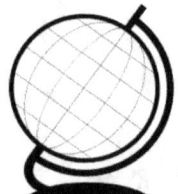
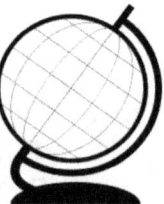

TRY DRAWING A GLOBE

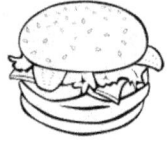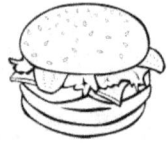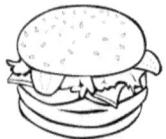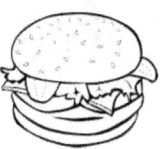

TRY DRAWING A HAMBURGER

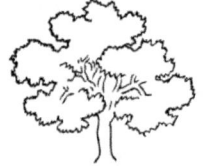
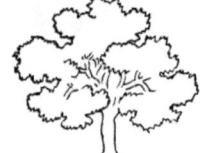
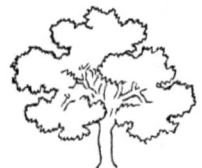
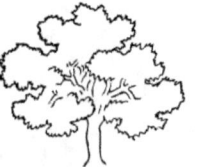

TRY DRAWING AN OAK TREE

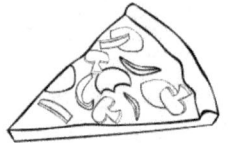
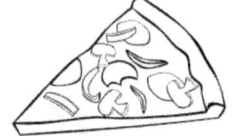
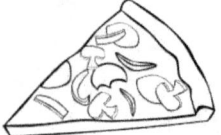
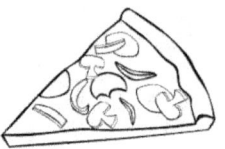

TRY DRAWING A PIZZA

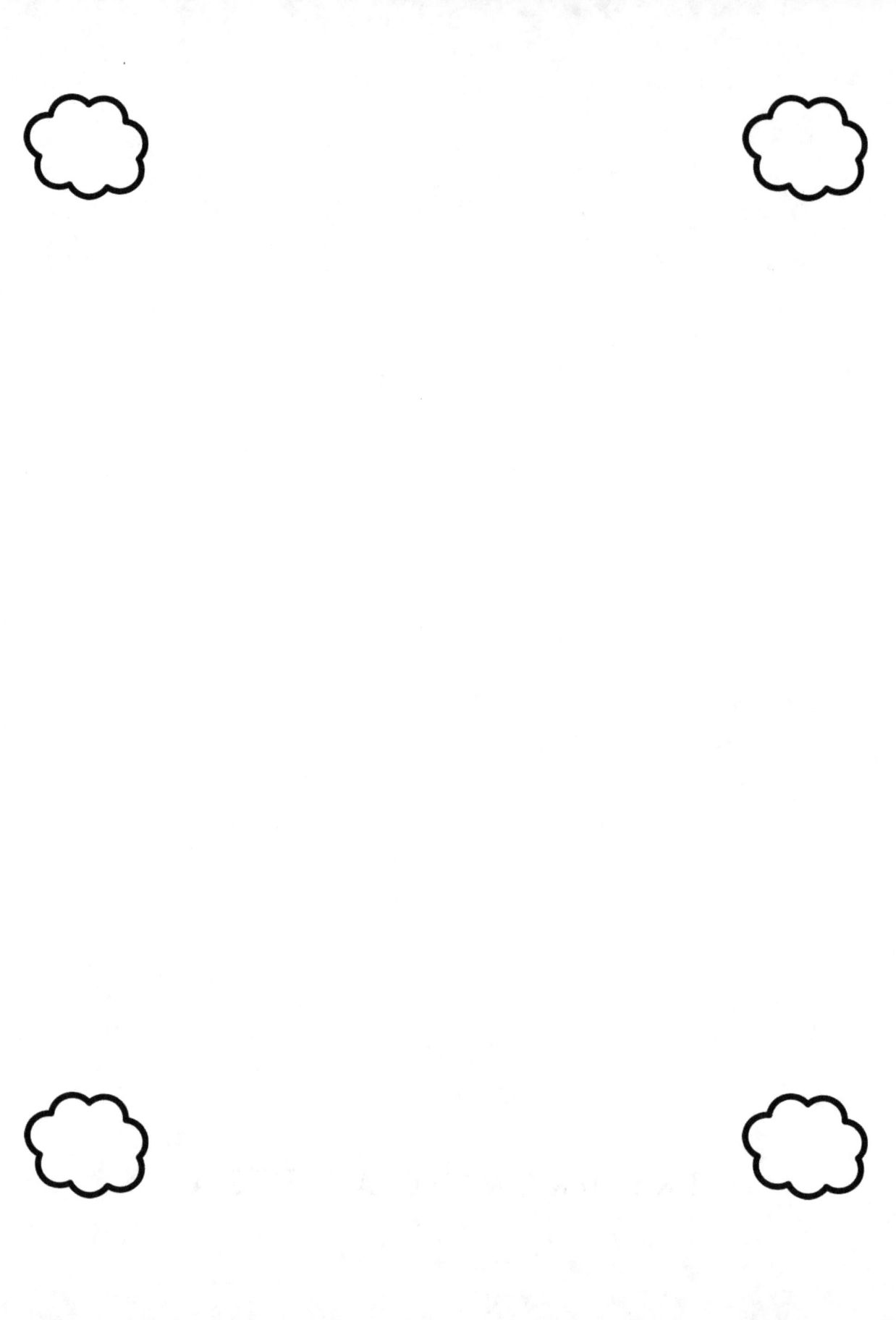

TRY DRAWING CLOUDS

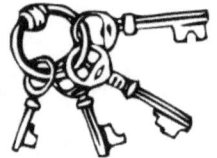
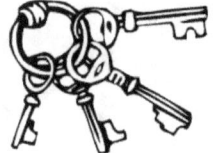
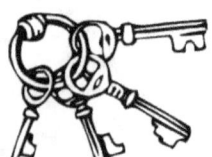
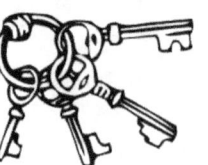

TRY DRAWING KEYS

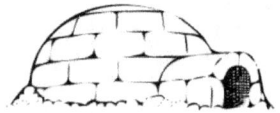
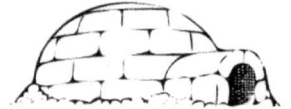
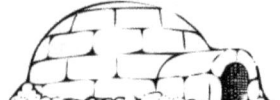
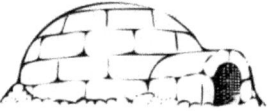

TRY DRAWING AN IGLOO

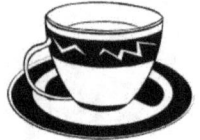
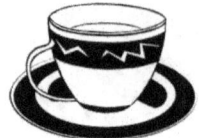
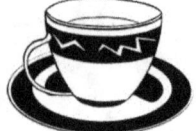
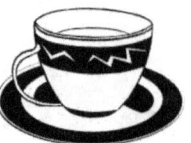

TRY DRAWING A TEA CUP

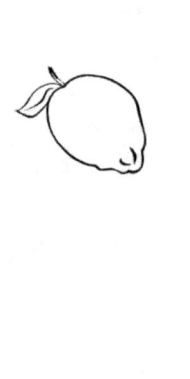
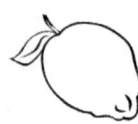
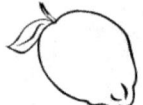
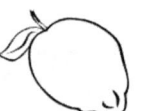

TRY DRAWING A LEMON

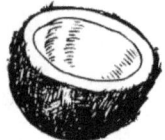
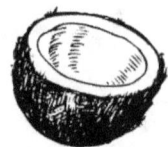
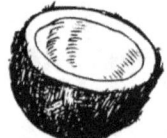
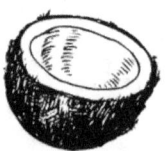

TRY DRAWING A COCONUT

TRY DRAWING AN OPENED BOOK

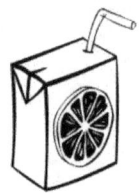
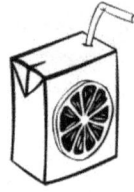
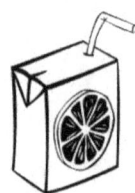
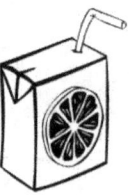

TRY DRAWING A JUICE BOX

TRY DRAWING GRAPES

TRY DRAWING A STAR

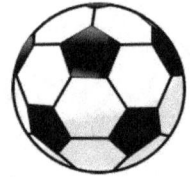
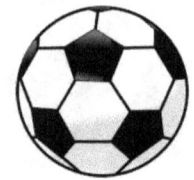
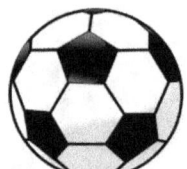
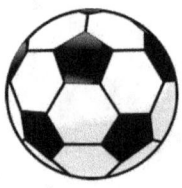

TRY DRAWING A SOCCER BALL

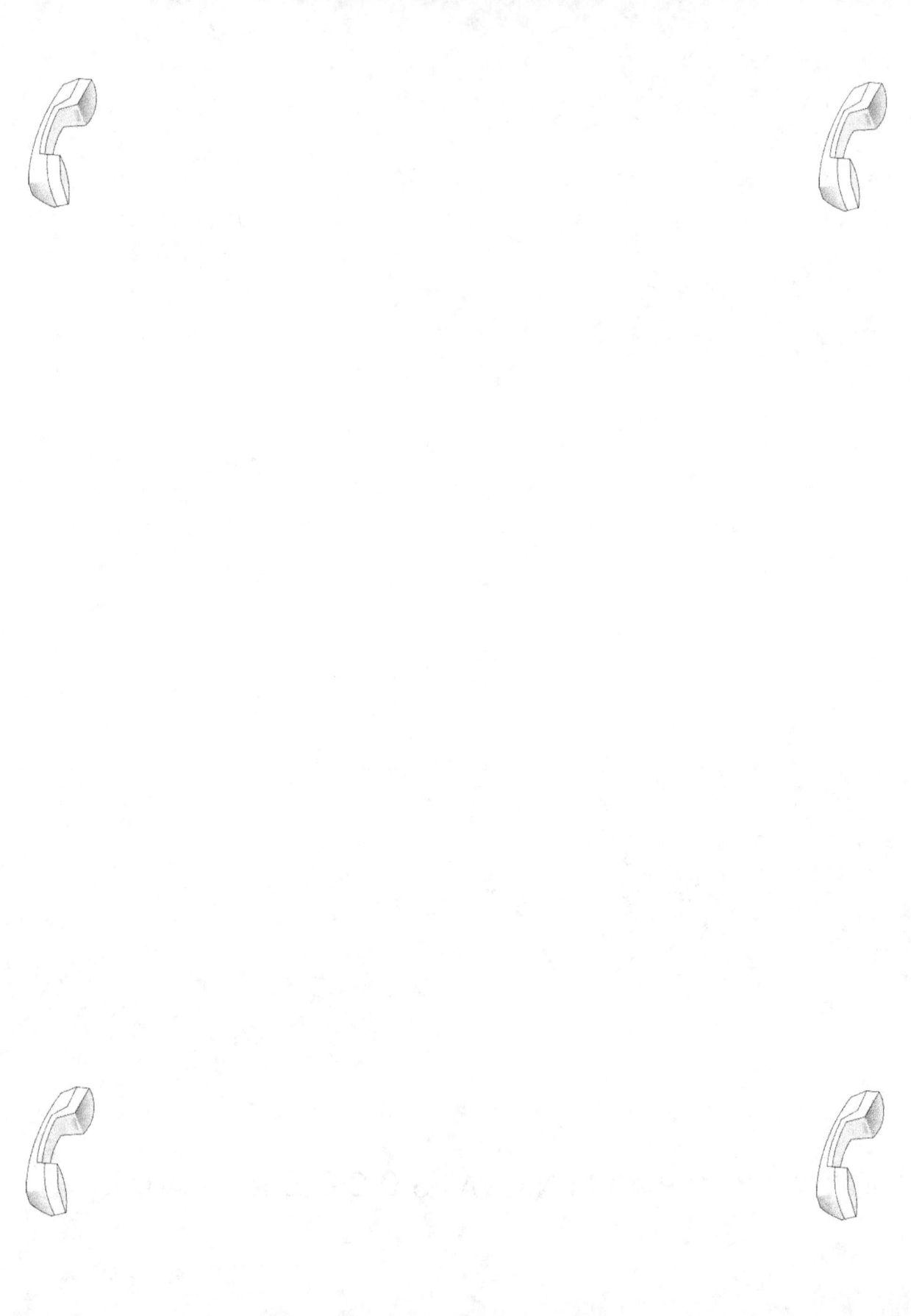

TRY DRAWING A HOME PHONE

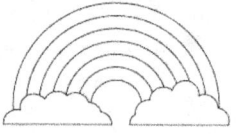
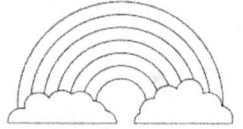
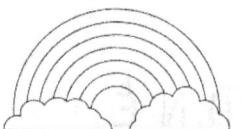
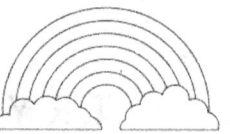

TRY DRAWING A RAINBOW

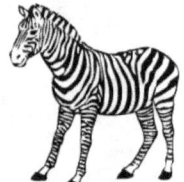
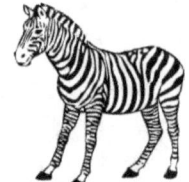
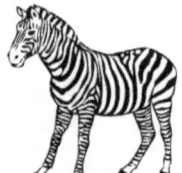
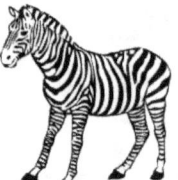

TRY DRAWING A ZEBRA

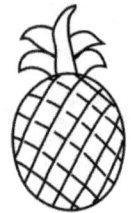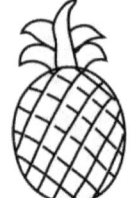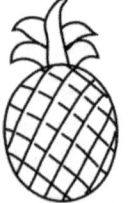

TRY DRAWING A PINEAPPLE

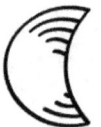

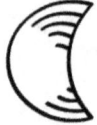
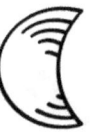

TRY DRAWING THE MOON

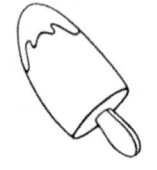
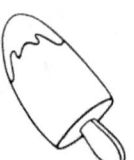
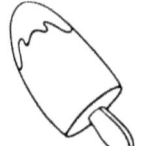
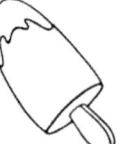

TRY DRAWING AN ICE POP